# of frogs & snails

**Finger Plays and Action Rhymes
For Children**

A BELAIR PUBLICATION

FIRST PUBLISHED IN GREAT BRITAIN 1986 BY
BELAIR PUBLICATIONS LTD.
P.O. BOX 12
TWICKENHAM
TW1 1NR
ENGLAND.
REPRINTED 1988.

PUBLISHED IN AUSTRALIA BY
BELAIR PUBLICATIONS PTY. LTD.
73 MADISON DRIVE,
ADAMSTOWN HEIGHTS,
N.S.W. 2289
AUSTRALIA.

TEXT © 1979 YVONNE WINER
ILLUSTRATIONS © 1979 LYNDALL STEWART

Designed and edited by DAVID E. CORNEY

This book is copyright. Apart from any fair dealing for the purposes of private study, research, criticism or review, as permitted under the Copyright Act, no part may be reproduced by any process without written permission. Inquiries should be addressed to the publishers.

ISBN 0 947882 05 7

# of frogs & snails

Finger Plays And Action Rhymes

by YVONNE WINER

Illustrations

by LYNDALL STEWART

FINGER PLAYS

Actions	41
African Elephant	42
Autumn Leaves	20
Busy Ants	40
Busy Fingers	10
Caterpillar, Where Will You Go	35
Clap Your Hands	14
Crackly Egg	13
Creepy Caterpillar	17
Creepy Crawly	34
Fingers Dance	10
Fingers Twinkle	8
Five Candles	33
Five Caterpillars	29
Five Little Eggs	13
Five Little Mice	21
Five Mice Sleeping	11
Flower Buds	28
Funny Bug	43
Golden Raindrops	39
Grandfather Snail	9
Great Big Bullfrog	32
Leaves	36
Little Thumb	16
Mice Creeping	11
My Hands	8
Percussion Band	24
Pussycat Creeping	18
Rabbits In The Tall Grass	38
Raindrops	23
Shiny Shells	37
Slippery Dip	23
Slippery Slidey Snake	30
Snip, Snip, Snip	15
Spider, Spider	22
Ten Little Fingers	16
These Two Rabbits	26
Things To Do	25
This Is The Rainbow	31
Three Old Snails	12
Two Little Birds	27
Two Tortoises	19
Wriggle Your Fingers	14

ACTION RHYMES

A Bee In My Garden	47
African Animals	60
Autumn Leaves	78
Blocks	46
"Cheep", Said The Bird	58
Crazy Crab	56
Down To The Pool	50
Elephants	70
Fairies In My Garden	75
Five Garden Snails	63
Five Green Frogs	52
Five Little Flowers	77
Five Stripy Socks	62
Funny Freddie Frog	69
Going Fishing	64
Golden Oranges	74
Good Morning	63
Horatio	66
I Sit On The Ground	55
Lady Beetle	53
Let's Play Shadows	71
Little Birds	72
Look Up In The Tree	51
My Umbrella	68
One Little Duck	65
See My Candle	67
Snails Crawling And Sliding	50
Tall Trees	61
The Circus	76
The Elf	79
The Pool	59
The Spinning Top	57
This Is The Sun	48
Toy Soldiers	73
Trees	49
Upon A Beach	57
Walking Tiptoe	54

SILLY VERSE

The Centipede	80
The Elephant	80
The Emu	80
The Monkey	80

THE VALUE OF FINGER PLAYS

Children delight in rhyme, especially when they can interpret it through simple body movement.

Finger Plays and Action Rhymes are used in the earlier years of speech development as a form of very simple dramatization. They are often used as a therapeutic aid with children suffering from speech difficulties. The child derives much pleasure from co-ordinating hand or body movement and verse. Throughout this book the verse is simple and the rhythm strong, aiding the teaching of clear pronunciation and rhythmic interpretation of motor co-ordination.

These verses lend themselves well to group experimentation in inflection and tone. For example, say the first part of the finger play **Five Candles** in normal tones and then whisper the last two lines, with exaggerated noises for the wind. In the same way some verses could be said in gruff voices, others could start quietly and end loudly.

Finger Plays and Action Rhymes are a pleasant means of communication between adult and child. They can be used to gain the attention of a noisy group of children and of those who have become disinterested or distracted. One or two Finger Plays at the beginning of a group activity, whether it be number, writing, music or poetry, is an excellent aid to attention. A quiet Finger Play at the end leaves the group relaxed.

As with all other activities associated with speech, this should be a time of enjoyment. Both Finger Plays and Action Rhymes are a form of dramatization, some requiring group participation, some requiring more individual response with group support. The children are not expected to respond in parrot-like fashion to the words. The words and finger play are introduced simultaneously, so that the words are supported by the action, facilitating an appreciation of the verse.

Where some of the Action Rhymes require one or a few children to dramatize the words, it is easier to first read the verse to the group so that they can become familiar with the contents. A discussion on possible interpretations should then follow. Children are creative at this age, and their vivid imagination, together with their own spontaneous interpretation, graceful movement and gesture can make this an interesting exercise in inventive group activity.

The suggestions in the notes beneath each verse are to act as guides only, since there are numerous ways in which the verses can be interpreted.

New subject matter can be introduced by a Finger Play or Action Rhyme, e.g., autumn leaves, African animals, numbers. Vocabulary is stimulated and new words are introduced in a familiar subject, e.g., **deciduous** trees. Words are more readily related to objects, e.g., giraffe—tall, ball—round.

When dramatizing the Action Rhymes, the teacher should be alert to the needs of each individual child in the group. The Finger Plays and Action Rhymes help to bring the shy, insecure children into a position where they can identify with the group in a familiar situation. They should be encouraged to participate but never forced into a situation for which they do not volunteer, where too much attention is focused upon them, or where demands are made beyond their ability.

For very young children there is also the achievement of coping with some Finger Plays which demand dexterous finger manipulation, e.g., **Two Tortoises,** or an exercise requiring them to bring forward one finger at a time from a clenched fist.

It is not possible to arrange the verse in this book in strict age order, since Finger Plays that are quite suitable for, say a three-year-old child from the point of view of rhyme, words and actions, can be equally suited to the more mature seven-year-old child from the point of view of the subject, interpretation and the jingle. The latter verses in each section are more suitable for children from four-and-a-half to seven years.

The subjects dealt with are within the experience of the three to seven-year-old child. They provide enjoyment, demand manipulative exercises of the fingers and gross motor co-ordination of the body, stimulate the imagination, and demand inventiveness. In these ways, they are useful aids in the all-round development of children.

Although this book has been written with groups of children in mind, both in Pre-schools and Infants Schools, it can be equally well adapted to the home situation.

finger plays

My Hands

I hide my hands,
I shake my hands,
I give a little clap.
I clap my hands,
I shake my hands,
I hide them in my lap.

ACTION: Translate words to actions.

Fingers Twinkle

Finger twinkle,
Fingers close,
Creep them, creep them,
To your nose!

Fingers twinkle,
Fingers close,
Crawl them, crawl them,
To your toes!

ACTION: Translate words to actions.

Grandfather Snail

Grandfather snail with his
Feelers out front.
Humpity, humpity, hump.
Over the pebbles,
Over the stump.
Humpity, humpity, hump!

ACTION:
    Line: 1 & 2 & 3. Extend right hand fore and middle
                    fingers to make a "snail".
          4. Right hand crawls over left hand.
          5. Right hand crawls over left arm.

Busy Fingers

Creep, busy fingers,
Creep, creep, creep!
Sleep, sleepy eyes,
Sleep, sleep, sleep!
Wake, sleepy eyes,
Open them wide!
Hide, busy fingers,
Hide, hide, hide!

ACTION: Translate words to actions.

Fingers Dance

My fingers dance
And hide away.
Crawl them out
And see them play.
Slowly, slowly, let them creep,
Fold them up and go to sleep.

ACTION:
Line: 1. Dance fingers.
2. Hide fingers behind back.
3. Crawl fingers along.
4. Dance fingers.
5. Creep fingers slowly.
6. Fold hands.

Mice Creeping

Small mice creeping
On soft mice feet,
Patter ... Patter .. Patter.

Pussy cat crawling
On pussy cat feet ......
Mice all scamper and scatter!

ACTION:
 Verse 1: Be right hand slowly creeping and crawling along (very quietly).
 Verse 2:
   Line: 1 & 2. Left hand with firm deliberate movements crawling.
       3. Right hand scampers away.

Five Mice Sleeping

Five mice sleeping
So quiet in their nest.
Wake one,
Wake two,
Wake up all the rest!

ACTION:
  Line: 1 & 2. Have hand clasped, all fingers tucked up.
       3. Hold up little finger.
       4. Hold up ring finger.
       5. Hold up the rest of fingers.

Three Old Snails

Three old snails sleeping,
They're curled up so small,
Sh....., Sh....., Sh.....
One wakes up slowly,
Crawl ...., crawl ...., crawl ....

Continue with

Two old snails sleeping ...
One old snail sleeping.

ACTION: Select three children to be "snails".
Verse 1:
   Line: 1 & 2. "Snails" curl up.
         3. Fingers on lips.
         4. "Feelers" i.e., arms extended.
         5. Shuffle on knees with arms extended.

Five Little Eggs

Five little eggs all speckled and white
Side by side in their nest.
Out popped the head of the first little chick!
Out popped the heads of the rest!

ACTION:
Line: 1. Extend fingers on right hand.
2. Cup hand, close fist.
3. Thumb pops out.
4. Other fingers pop out, one by one.
Repeat with left hand.

Crackly Egg

Little chicken in the egg,
Quiet as quiet can be.
Crackle, crackle, crackle, crack,
Out pops she!

ACTION:
Line: 1 & 2. Clench thumb in fist.
3. Rotate fist back and forth.
4. Thumbs pop out.

Wriggle Your Fingers

Wriggle your fingers,
Wriggle your toes.
Stand your soldiers (fingers)
In two straight rows.
Hide your fingers,
Hide your toes.
No more soldiers
In two straight rows!

ACTION: Translate words to actions.

Clap Your Hands

Clap your hands,
Twist them round.
Touch the sky,
Touch the ground.

Clap your hands,
Stamp your feet.
Nod your head,
Go to sleep.

ACTION: Translate words into actions.

Snip, Snip, Snip

I take my scissors—
SNIP, SNIP, SNIP!—
And cut the paper
Into bits!

Some are round,
Some are square,
Some have patterns
Everywhere!

ACTION:
  Verse 1: Right hand is "scissors". Left hand is "paper". Snip with extended first and second fingers on right hand.
  Verse 2:
    Line: 1 & 2. Using both hands, press thumb and forefingers together making rounds and squares.
    3 & 4. Put left hand over right. Make lattice patterns with extended fingers.

Ten Little Fingers

Ten little fingers standing up tall.
Hide away fingers, hide away all!
Here comes thumbkin creeping out,
See him nod and dance about!

Continue with

Here comes pointer creeping out ...
Here comes tall man creeping out ...
Here come ringman creeping out ...
Here comes baby creeping out ...

ACTION:
  Line: 1. Hold up both hands, fingers extended.
     2. Hide fingers behind back.
     3. Thumb creeps out.
     4. Thumb dances about.

Little Thumb

Little thumb can stand up straight,
So very, very tall!
Little thumb can hide away,
Now he is very small!
Little thumb can dance about,
And bounce this way and that.
Clap your hands! Fold your hands!
Put them in your lap.

ACTION: Translate words to actions.

Creepy Caterpillar

Creepy, crawly, caterpillar,
In my garden small.
See him crawling, crawling, crawling,
Up the garden wall.

Creepy, crawly, caterpillar,
On the garden wall.
See him crawling back again,
To my garden, small.

ACTION:
  Verse 1:
    Line: 1 & 2. Pointer finger on right hand rests and wiggles on palm of left hand.
        3. Crawls up the left arm.
        4. Rests on shoulder.
  Verse 2:
    Line: 1 & 2. Pointer finger resting on shoulder.
        3. Crawls down arm.
        4. Rests in palm of hand.

Pussycat Creeping

Pussycat creeping and crawling along.
Little bird chirping a gay little song.
Up jumps pussy, right into the tree!
Away flies the bird so glad to be free!

ACTION:
    Line: 1. Right hand fingers creeping along.
           2. Left hand sitting on left shoulder.
           3. Right hand on to left shoulder.
           4. Left hand flies away.

Two Tortoises

Two old tortoises
Going for a walk.

"Good morning", said one,
"Shall we have a little talk?"

"Yes", said the other,
"I do enjoy a chat".

So they walked along together
With a natter, natter, nat!

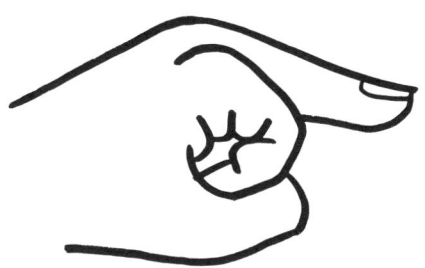 

ACTION:
- Line: 1 & 2. Clenched fists with second fingers extended, moving slowly forward.
- 3 & 4. Both hands stop, right hand extended finger wiggles. (Voice deliberate and a little gruff).
- 5 & 6. Left hand extended finger wiggles.
- 7 & 8. Both hands moved forwards, with extended fingers wiggling.

Leaves

Little leaves, little leaves,
High up in the trees.
Little leaves, little leaves,
Swinging in the breeze.
Autumn comes along
And they change from red to brown.
Winter comes along,
And they flutter to the ground.

ACTION:
    Line: 1 & 2. Hands "flutter" above head.
           3 & 4. Arms outstretched sideways—hands flutter.
           5 & 6. Arms outstretched, palms up, palms down.
           7 & 8. Hands flutter gently to the ground.

Five Little Mice

Five little mice went creeping,
Creeping in the night.

Big black puss lay sleeping,
Sleeping, in the quiet.

Suddenly our puss woke up,
And started at a pace!

Little mice ran faster, though,
And easily won the race!

ACTION:
 Line: 1 & 2. Five fingers on right hand are mice creeping.
 3 & 4. Left hand is puss curled up.
 5 & 6. Left hand bounces in direction of right hand.
 7 & 8. Right hand fingers scuttle behind back.

Spider, Spider

Spider hurrying,
Spider scurrying,
See her silken thread.
Spider hurrying,
Spider scurrying,
See her little web!

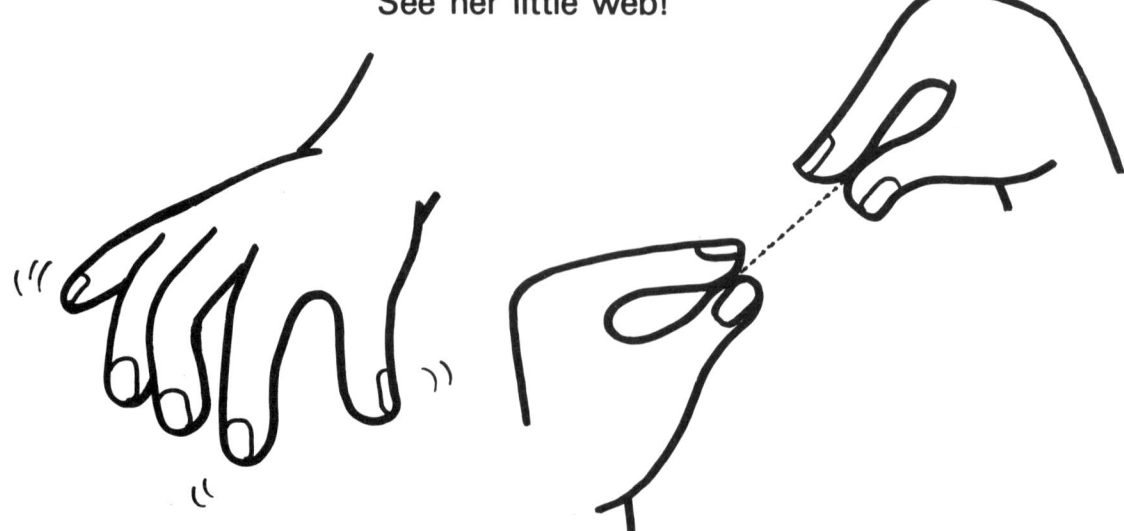

ACTION:
Line: 1 & 2. Run fingers back and forth.
3. Stretch imaginary thread between forefingers and thumbs.
4 & 5. Run fingers back and forth.
6. Make spiral with forefingers.

Raindrops

Raindrops glisten,
Raindrops sparkle,
Raindrops fall and crash!
See them glimmer,
See them shimmer,
See them fall and splash!

ACTION:
Line: 1 & 2. "Twinkle" fingers.
3. Roll arms and clap hands on "crash".
4 & 5. "Twinkle" fingers.
6. Roll arms and clap hands on "splash".

The Slippery Dip

Little boy climbing, and climbing, and climbing,
Step by step to the top!
Ready to go—fast as he can—
He slides to the ground with a FLOP!

ACTION:
Line: 1 & 2. Use first and second finger on right hand to climb up left arm.
3. Rest right hand on left shoulder.
4. Slide down arm. Thump on floor.
Repeat with left hand.

Percussion Band

Hush, hush, everybody!
What do you hear?
Drum, drum, a-drum, drumming,
The big drum is near!

Hush, hush, everybody!
What do you hear?
Toot, toot, a-toot, tooting,
The bugle is near!

Hush, hush, everybody!
What do you hear?
Clang, clang, a-clang, clanging,
The cymbals are near!

Hush, hush, everybody!
What do you hear?
Ting, ting, a-ling, linging,
The triangles are near.

ACTION:
  Verse 1:
   Line: 1. First finger to lips (right hand).
       2. Hand to ear (left hand).
    3 & 4. Play imaginary drum.
         Continue in same way with other verses. Encourage children to suggest new instruments.

Things To Do

I've two little hands
They're hiding away.
Now here comes one
—and the other—to play!

They are so good for clapping,
And shaking, and tapping,
For rolling, and pushing,
And kneading, and pulling!
They are quite good for pointing
To the left, or the right,
And ever so easy, to fold up at night!

ACTION:
Verse 1:
    Line: 1 & 2. Both hands behind back.
        3. Right hand appears.
        4. Left hand appears.
Verse 2: Hand movements to suit words.

These Two Rabbits

These two rabbits
Have ears so tall.

These two rabbits
Have eyes so small.

These two rabbits
Have whiskers that wiggle.

These two rabbits
Have noses that wriggle.

These two rabbits, the smallest of all,
Curl up tightly in a round furry ball.

ACTION:
- Line: 1. Hold up thumbs.
    2. Hands above head.
    3. First fingers.
    4. Point to eyes.
    5. Second fingers.
    6. Five fingers on each hand extended away from thumbs, against face, to make whiskers.
    7. Third fingers.
    8. Point to nose.
    9. Small fingers.
    10. Fold hands together.

Two Little Birds

Two little birds, up in the sky.
Two little butterflies, fluttering by.
Two little fish, in a pool so deep.
Two little children, fast asleep.

ACTION:
    Line: 1. Point to sky.
          2. Fly with arms.
          3. Hands together.
          4. Hands against face in "sleeping" position.

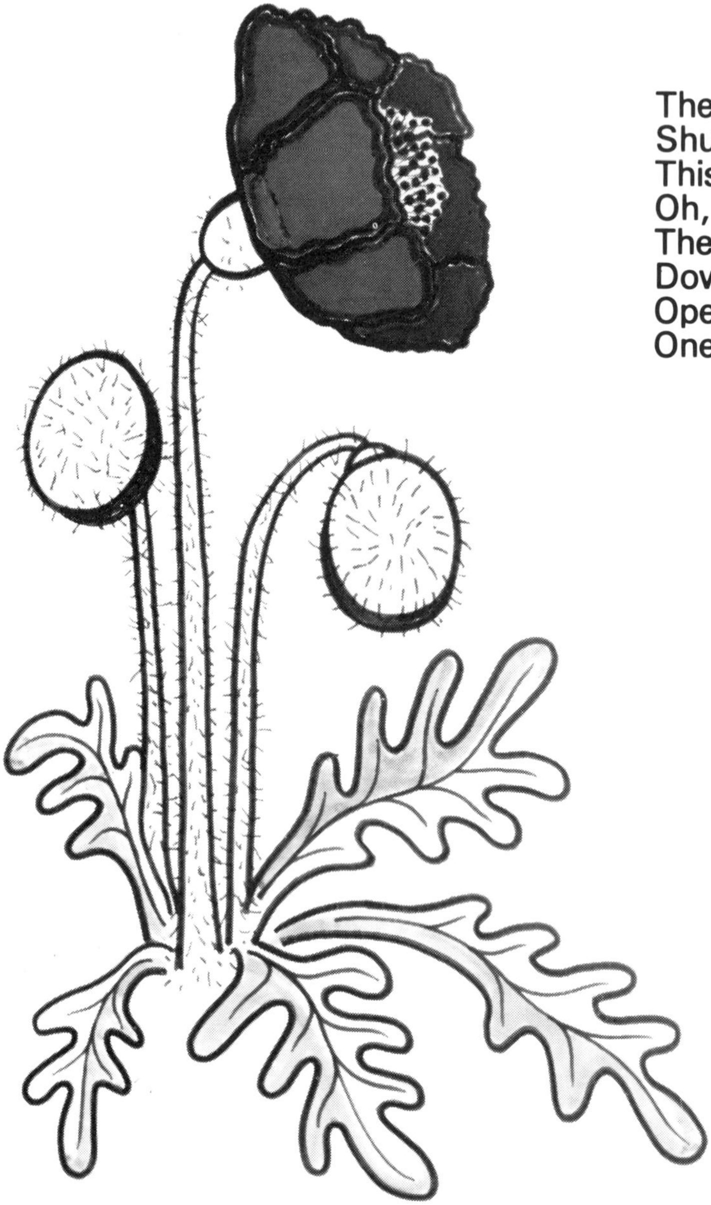

Flower Buds

These are the flower buds,
Shut so tight.
This is the sun,
Oh, so bright!
These are the rain drops,
Down they come.
Open, flowers,
One by one!

ACTION:
    Line: 1 & 2. Right hand clenched.
           3 & 4. Left hand above head.
           5 & 6. Both hands come down as rain.
           7 & 8. Right hand, then left hand, slowly unfolds.

Five Caterpillars

Five caterpillars,
Where have they gone?
Hiding away,
All day long!

Five caterpillars,
Here they come.
Wriggly, squiggly,
One by one.

ACTION:
 Verse 1: Fist folded tight.
 Verse 2: Unfold fingers one by one and wiggle hand along floor.

Slippery Slidey Snake

Slippery slidey snake,
Basking in the sun.
Caught five little beetles,
One by one.

Silly, silly snake,
Forgot to swallow them.
1, 2, 3, 4, 5, jolly beetles,
All crept out again.

ACTION:
Verse 1:
    Line: 1 & 2. Right arm lies quietly, right hand is to look like snake head.
          3 & 4. Left hand is five little beetles which are "eaten" by right hand.
Verse 2:
    Line: 1 & 2. Left hand "nestles" in right hand.
          3 & 4. Left hand slowly withdraws and runs away!

This Is The Rainbow

This is the rainbow, with colours so gay,
That bridges the sky, when the sun comes to play.

This is the cloud, that is heavy and black,
That falls down as rain with a pit-a-pat, pat.

This is the moon that shines in the night,
And these are the stars, all twinkling bright.

ACTION:
    Line:
1. Sweep right hand through air, above head.
2. Left hand fingers outstretched above head.
3. Both hands, pushed upwards, palms up.
4. Fingers run down as rain.
5. Arms in circle, hands clasped above head.
6. Both hands "twinkle" as stars.

Great Big Bullfrog

Great big bullfrog
Sitting on the ground
Watches five mosquitoes,
Buzzing round and round ...
   zzz   zzz   zzz

Then with a jump, a hop, and a leap
He catches one mosquito
And goes to sleep.

       Continue with

    Watches four mosquitoes ...
    Watches three mosquitoes ...
    Watches two mosquitoes ...
    Watches one mosquito ...

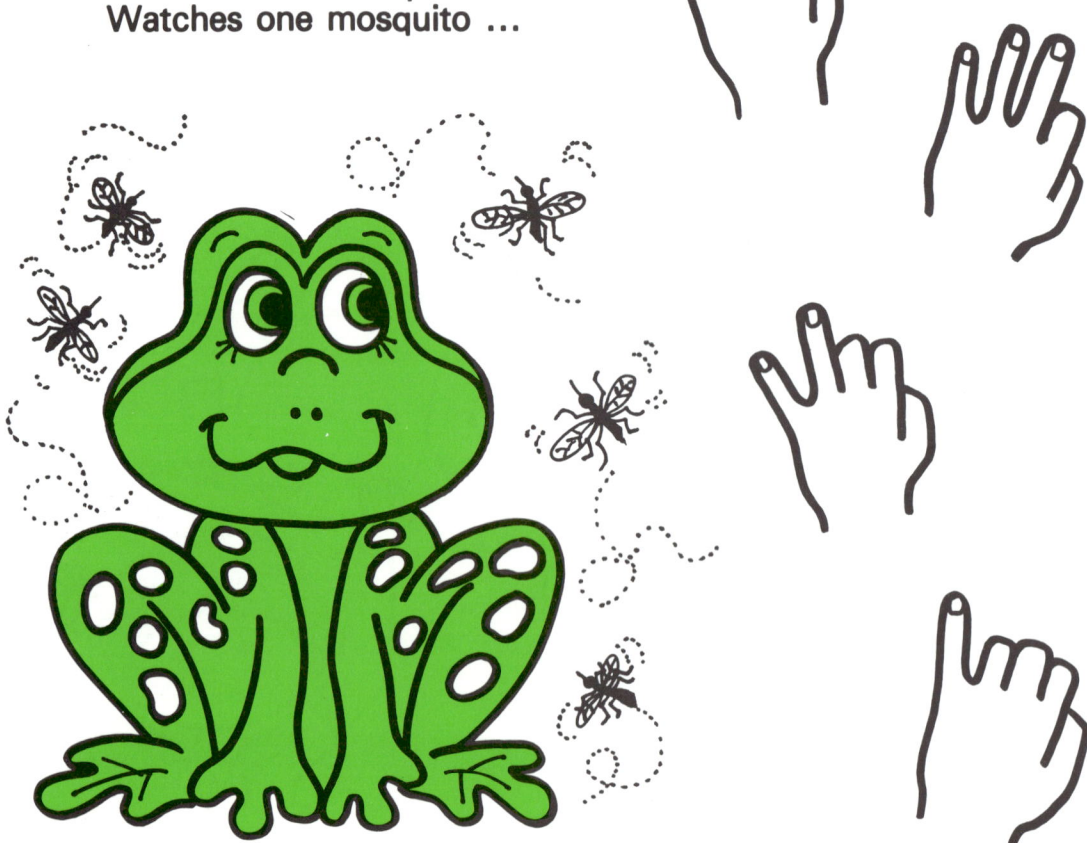

ACTION: One hand, fist clenched, is bullfrog sleeping. Other hand, open fingers extended, is mosquitoes. Fold up one finger on "mosquito" hand as each "mosquito" is caught. Follow verse for bullfrog actions.

Five Candles

Five little candles in the night.
Five little candles, burning bright.
Along comes the wind...............
Shooooooooooo...............All is quiet.
Four little candles
Burning in the night!

Continue with

Four little candles ...
Three little candles ...
Two little candles ...
One little candle ...

ACTION:
  Line: 1 & 2. Extend fingers on right hand.
   3. Left hand comes along.
   4. Shoooooooooooo.
   5. Fold down one finger.
   6. Leave four fingers extended.
    Repeat and fold away another finger with each verse.

33

Creepy Crawly

Creepy crawly up my arm.
A spotty little bug!
When he crawls up to my neck,
I give a little shrug!

But, ... he climbs a little more
And settles on my nose,
So I give a mighty SNORE!
And he scuttles to my toes.

ACTION: Verse 1:
    Line: 1 & 2. Creep fingers up left arm.
           3. Creep fingers up neck.
           4. Shrug.
  Verse 2:
    Line: 1 & 2. Creep fingers to nose.
           3. SNORE — loudly.
           4. Run fingers to toes.

Caterpillar, Where Will You Go?

Caterpillar, caterpillar,
Where will you go?
Up and down the branches
To where the flowers grow.

Caterpillar, caterpillar,
What will you do?
I'll spin my cocoon
And then rest too.

Caterpillar, caterpillar,
Why, why, why?
Because you see
I'm to be a butterfly!

ACTION:
  Verse 1: 1 & 2. Look at forefinger.
         3. Run finger up and down arm.
         4. Rest finger in palm and touch other fingers (flowers).
  Verse 2:
    Line: 1 & 2. Look at finger.
          3 & 4. Clench fist and use other hand to spin an imaginary thread round the fist.
  Verse 3:
    Line: 1 & 2. Look at fist.
          3 & 4. Link thumbs to make "butterfly". Spread and flap other fingers.

Autumn Leaves

Up in a tree,
All is so quiet,
Five autumn leaves,
Yellow and bright.

Whoo ...... hear the wind blow,
Whooo ..... hear the wind sigh,
Blow one autumn leaf
Into the sky!

Repeat with 4, 3, 2, 1.

ACTION:
　Verse 1:
　　Line: 1 - 5. Hold up right hand and gently sway.
　Verse 2:
　　Line: 1 & 2. Make sound and wave left hand.
　　　　　3 & 4. "Blow" fingers on right hand into the air.

Shiny Shells

Shiny, tiny, silvery shells,
Lying in the sand.
Pick them up, dust them off,
Hold them in your hand.

How many have you?
Can you say?
One, two, three, four, five,
Today!

ACTION:
Verse 1:
  Line: 1 & 2. Fingers twinkle.
        3 & 4. Translate words to action.
Verse 2:
  Line: 1 & 2. Open left hand and look at palm.
  Count the fingers one by one.

Rabbits In The Tall Grass

Rabbits in the tall grass,
Possums in the trees.
Birds up in the blue sky,
Hives of busy bees—
Bzzzzzzz.

ACTION:
    Line: 1. Use both hands for rabbit ears, then stretch up arms for tall grass.
        2. Sway, with arms outstretched for trees.
        3. Flap arms.
        4. Hands clenched above head, arms forming hive.
        5. Fingers flying about as bees.

Golden Raindrops

Golden raindrops, golden raindrops,
What a merry sight!
See them sparkle just like dew drops,
Just like diamonds, shiny bright.

How they bounce, and splash, and glimmer,
And make patterns on the pane.
There's gentle tinkling music
In the sound of falling rain!

ACTION:
 Verse 1: Translate words into finger movements.
 Verse 2:
   Line: 1. Hand movement to suit words.
         2. Make "patterns" with fingers.
         3. Put hand to ear, listen.
         4. Hands floating down—"rain".

Busy Ants

Busy ants are everywhere!
Up the tree,
And down the stairs.
Hiding in the garden hose,
And even biting at MY toes!

ACTION:
　　Line: 1. Fingers are ants scuttling everywhere.
　　　　 2. Run up arm and shoulder.
　　　　 3. Run down body to knee.
　　　　 4. Peck up sleeve.
　　　　 5. Touch toes.

Actions

Tall grass waving,
Waving in the breeze.
Big ships sailing,
Sailing on the seas.
Little fish swimming,
Swimming in the deep.
Little children nodding,
Falling fast asleep.

ACTION:
    Line: 1 & 2. Hands wave above head.
           3 & 4. Make "steeple" shape above head with arms and sway.
           5 & 6. Hands together in front "swimming".
              7. Nod heads.
              8. Hands under chin, fall asleep.

The African Elephant

The elephant has enormous ears,
And a trunk so very long.
His eyes are very tiny, though,
And his tusks are sharp and strong.

ACTION:
  Line: 1. Hands on either side of head, making ears.
     2. Hands together, arms outstretched in front.
     3. Point to eyes.
     4. Arms forward, curved upwards.

A Funny Bug

Once there was a bug,
With eyes SO round,
Her smile was very friendly,
And ... she never made a sound .....

She looked to the left ......,
And she looked to the right ......,
And then she made CROSS-EYES.
What a very funny sight!

ACTION:
Verse 1:
    Line: 1. Point to self.
          2. Make circles with fingers over eyes.
          3. Point to smiling mouth.
          4. Place "pointer" finger on lips.

Verse 2:
    Line: 1. Look to left.
          2. Look to right.
          3. Make cross-eyes.

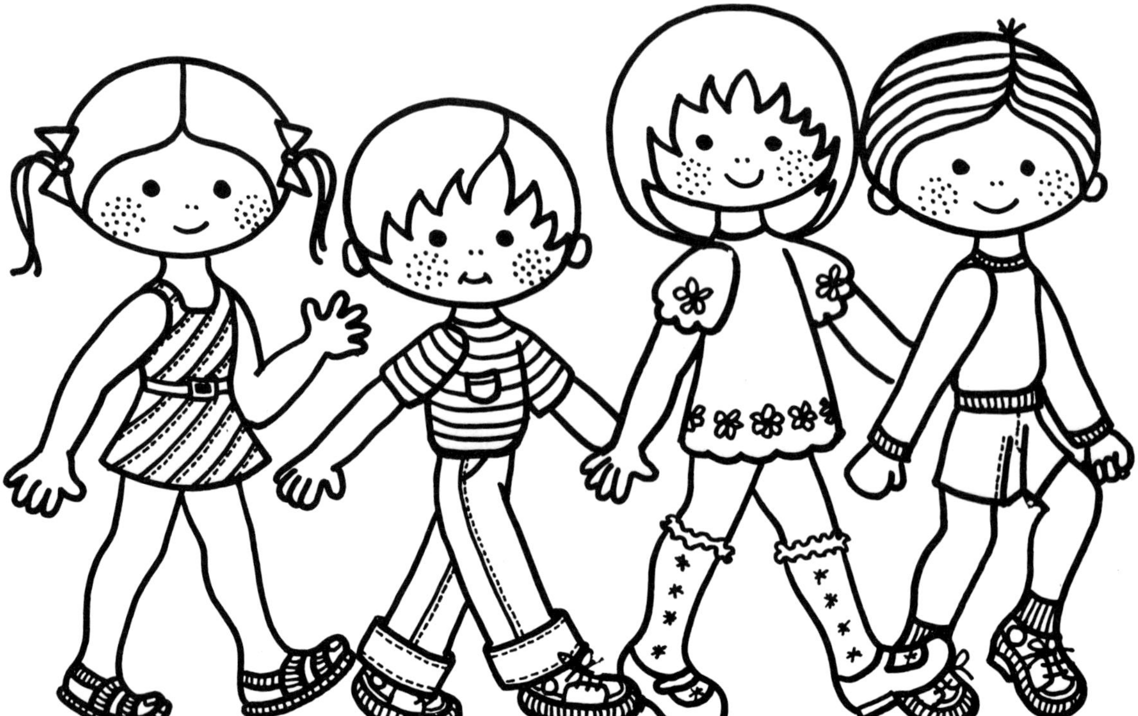

action rhymes

Blocks

I love to build a tower
With blocks so bright and gay.
These blocks are shiny red,
And these are blue and grey.
Up and up and up,
It's very, very tall.......

—Just one little push,
and DOWN THEY FALL!

ACTION: Start in a kneeling position.
    Line: 1 & 2. Place hands one above the other.
          3. Take an imaginary block from left.
          4. Take an imaginary block from right.
          5. Continue placing hands one above the other until in a standing position.
          6. Push.
          7. Roll hands down, then fall.
             Equally suitable as a finger play.

A Bee In My Garden

There's a bee in my garden,
It's buzzing away ...... zzz.
I wonder where it will find
Nectar today?

ACTION: Children sit in circle. One child is the bee and moves around. When the verse stops the bee touches the nearest child and that child becomes the next bee.

This Is The Sun

This is the sun
So big and round.
This is a seed
Snug in the ground.
These are the flowers
That wave in the breeze.
These are the yachts
That sail on the seas.

ACTION:
    Line: 1 & 2. Arms encircled above the head.
           3 & 4. Curl up and lie on the ground.
           5 & 6. Arms and fingers outstretched above the head.
           7 & 8. Place left hand on the hip, and right hand above the head walking round slowly.

Trees

There are trees in my garden,
Some big, and some small,
Some very bushy,
Some very tall.

Some bear berries and flowers so gay,
Some have thorns that are sharp and grey.
Others are—well—DECIDUOUS trees,
They lose their leaves in the cool Autumn breeze!

ACTION:
Verse 1:
   Line: 1. Children stand about being "trees".
   2. Stretch up, crouch down.
   3. Arms out to the side.
   4. Point up on tiptoe.
Verse 2:
   Line: 1. Make "berries" and "flowers" with hand shapes, in all directions.
   2. Whole body rigid, fingers out stiffly.
   3 & 4. Arms outstretched, sway from side to side.

Down To The Pond

Down to the pond,
The ducks all go.
Waddle, waddle, waddle,
Oh, so slow.

Down to the pond,
What fun! What fun!
Faster, faster, faster, faster,
Run, run, run.

ACTION: Select several children to be the ducks.
  Verse 1: Children squat, place hands on hips and "waddle" slowly.
         (Verse to be recited S-L-O-W-L-Y).
  Verse 2: Say verse a bit faster and increase tempo — ducks waddle faster and faster.

Snail Crawling And Sliding

Little snail crawling and sliding,
Little snail stopping ..... and hiding.
Then .... out come his feelers
Ever so slow .....,
Slide, slide, slide ...,
Where will he go?

ACTION:
  Line: 1. Right hand (or left) with fore and middle finger extended slide along.
      2. Right hand curls into fist.
      3. Forefinger and middle finger extends.
      4. Hand moves along.

Look Up In The Tree

Look up in the tree,
And what do you see?
A wagtail, a wren, and currawongs, three.
Gone are the wagtail and wren from the tree.
Gone too the currawongs,
One, two, three!

ACTION: Choose one child to look up in the "tree".
Choose five to be the birds.
They respond to the appropriate lines.

Five Green Frogs

Five green frogs.
Five green frogs.
Where can they be?
Hiding away,
Hiding away,
Hiding away
From me!

Five green frogs.
Five green frogs.
Time for a swim.
1, 2, 3, 4, 5,
They all jump in!

ACTION: Select five children to be frogs. Draw a "pond" and let children crouch round it with hands covering heads (Hiding!).
Verse 1: Children crouch down in hiding position.
Verse 2:
    Line: 1 & 2. Remain crouching.
           3. All bob heads up eagerly.
           4 & 5. Each takes a turn to jump into the pond.

Lady Beetle

In a tree ....
Behind a leaf ....
A lady beetle sat!

First .... she stuck her feelers out .....
Then .... she peered around ....
And then she moved her little legs and
Scuttled to the ground!

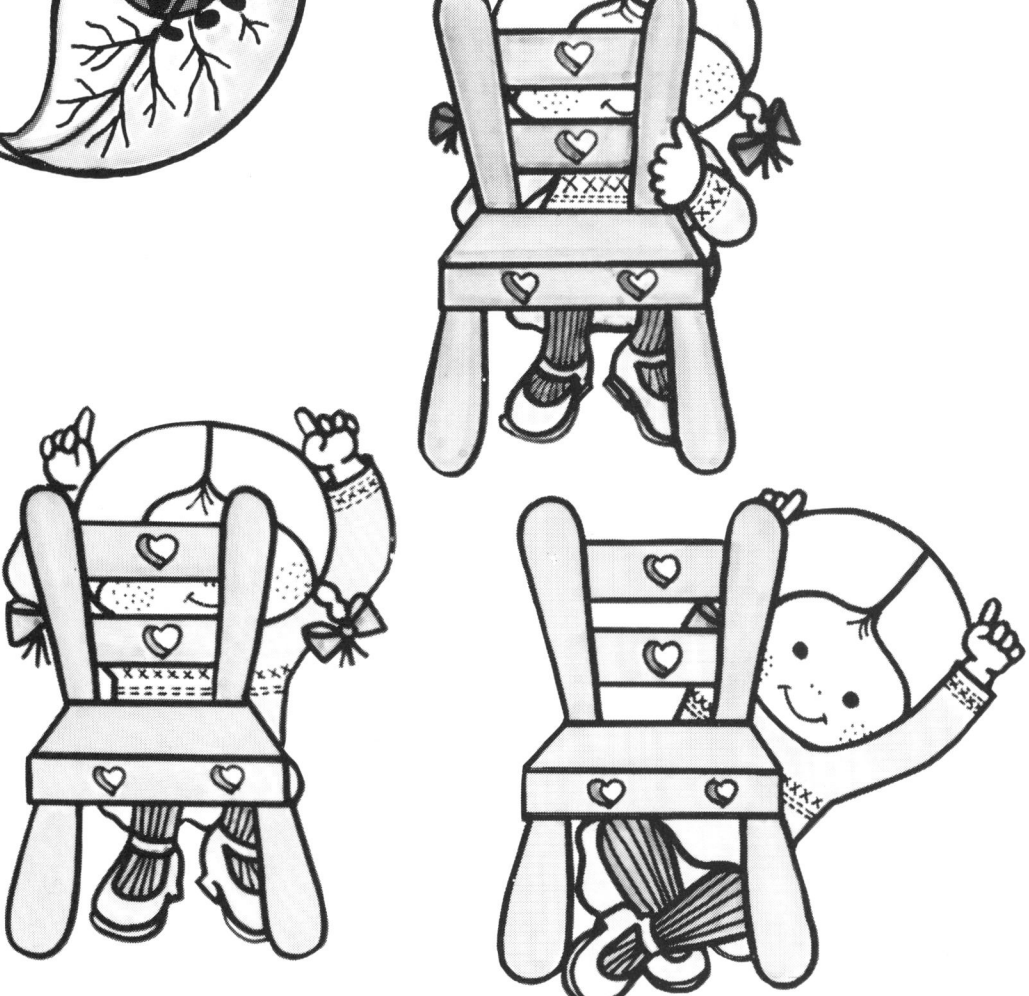

ACTION:
  Verse 1: Say very deliberately and slowly.
    Line: 1 & 2 & 3. A child hides behind a chair (carton, anything).
  Verse 2: Slowly bring feelers forward (arms), then poke head around, increase tempo
    and scurry about.

Walking Tiptoe

When I walk on tiptoe,
That makes me feel so tall.
When I crouch down low,
I feel so very small.
But what I like
The best of all [*hesitate for a while*]
Is to bounce, bounce, bounce,
Like a great big ball.

ACTION: Translate words to actions.

I Sit On The Ground

I sit on the ground,
I stand up tall,
I bounce and I bounce
Like a big round ball.
I clap my hands
And I nod my head—
I switch off the light
And I go to bed.

ACTION: The whole group or individual children respond to the words.

Crazy Crabs

Crazy crabs walk sideways,
What a giddy way to go!
Snails slip slide forwards
And that is very slow!

Ducks waddle, waddle,
And that is funny too,
And what about the hopping
Of the big Red Kangaroo?

ACTION: Translate words to actions.

Upon A Beach

Upon a beach
Three small shells lay,
And saw the water
Come out to play.

But, all the waves
Went back to sea,
And took those shells,
One, two and three.

ACTION: Children sit in a circle. Choose three children to be shells. Five others to be waves, holding hands.
Verse 1:
　Line: 1 & 2. Three shells lie on the beach.
　　　　3 & 4. The "waves" come and skip around them.
Verse 2: The waves take the shells by the hand and take them back to the sea.

The Spinning Top

I am a spinning top,
Round and round I go.
Sometimes, faster, faster, faster!
Sometimes very slow.
But, when I'm not spinning round at all,
Then down I fall!

ACTION: Translate words to body movement.

"Cheep," Said The Bird

"Cheep," said the bird
As she sat in the tree.
"Cheep," said the bird,
"Watch me!"
And she nodded her head
And she flapped her wings
And away flew she!

"Grump," said the frog
As he sat on a rock.
"Grump," said the frog,
"Watch me!"
And he nodded his head
And he stretched his legs
And away jumped he!

"Neigh," said the horse
As she stood in a field.
"Neigh," said the horse,
"Watch me!"
And she shook her head
And she stamped her feet
And away galloped she!

ACTION: This can be a group activity or individual children can be selected to interpret the words into actions. The verses are recited by the group. Continue the poem with other animals suggested by the children.

The Pool

In a pool
So quiet and deep,
Small fish swim,
And small crabs creep.

The Octopus
With arms so wide,
Sways around
From side to side.

ACTION: Translate words to actions.

African Animals

Giraffe are tall, with necks so long.
Elephants' trunks are big and strong.
Zebras have stripes and can gallop away,
While monkeys in the trees do sway.
Old crocodile swims in the pool so deep,
Or lies in the sun and goes to sleep.

ACTION:
- Line: 1. Arms stretched above head, tiptoe.
  2. Bend forward, arms down, hands together, swaying.
  3. Gallop.
  4. Move from "tree" to "tree", with swaying movement.
  5. Lie on ground and swim.
  6. Sleep.
  This can be for a group, or for a few selected children.

Tall Tree

I am a tall, tall, tall, tall, tree.
Leaves so round all cover me!
I am a tall, tall, tall, tall, tree.
Leaves so round all fall from me.

Repeat with: Leaves so thin.
Leaves so lumpy.
Leaves so spikey.

ACTION:
Line: 1. Starting in a crouched position grow and stretch to be a tall tree.
2. Make full arm movements to indicate shape of leaf.
3. Stretch up again to tall tree.
4. Slowly drop to ground.

Five Stripy Socks

Five stripy socks
On a line one day,
Sway, sway, sway.
A breeze came along (Anne!)
And took one away,
Sway, sway, sway.

Four stripy socks
On a line one day,
Sway, sway, sway.
A breeze came along (Sam!)
And took one away,
Sway, sway, sway.

Continue with

Three stripy socks ...
Two stripy socks ...
One stripy sock ...

ACTION: Five children are selected to be the socks. One child is called out at each verse to be the breeze and removes one "sock" from the line.

Five Garden Snails

Five garden snails
Sleeping in the sun.
Along comes a yellow bird (Jan)
And flies away with one!

Four garden snails
Sleeping in the sun.
Along comes a green bird (Peter)
And flies away with one.

Continue with Three garden snails ...
Two garden snails ...
One garden snail.

ACTION: Select five children to be the "Snails".
  Verse 1:
    Line: 1 & 2. Snails lie curled up sleeping.
         3. Select a child from the group wearing appropriate colour to fly along and fly away with a snail.

Good Morning

In the morning when I wake
I give a great big yawn,
I stretch my sleepy legs,
And stretch up both my arms!

Then I dress most hurriedly,
And wash my hands and face,
I brush my teeth and comb my hair,
Put on my shoe, tie my lace.
Eat my breakfast, drink milk so cool,
Wave to all—I'm off to school.

ACTION: Translate words into action.

Going Fishing

I took my shiny fishing rod
And went down to the sea.
There I caught a little fish,
Which made ....
One fish and me.

I took my shiny fishing rod
And went down to the sea.
There I caught a little crab,
Which made ......?
One fish, one crab and me.

I took my shiny fishing rod
And went down to the sea.
There I caught a little clam,
Which made ......?
One fish, one crab, one clam
.... and me!

GOING FISHING
GAME: Have a box of assorted sea animals cut out of stiff card with paper clips attached. Prepare a rod with magnet attached to string. Each child takes a turn to catch the sea creatures suggested in the verse.

One Little Duck

One little duck went waddling
And quacked as she went along.
She asked a little playmate
To join her merry song!

Two little ducks went waddling
And quacked as they went along.
They asked a little playmate
To join their merry song!

Three little ducks went waddling
And quacked as they went along.
But they could not find a playmate
To join their merry song.

ACTION: One child is selected to be the duck and waddles off quacking. This child selects another who follows single file. Continue until several ducks are in line and then end with last verse. The last child in the line always selects the next duck.

Horatio

Horatio is a mighty snake,
Who curls up very small.
But if he stretches up and up,
He really grows quite tall.

He loves to squiggle, slide and squirm,
And sway from side to side,
And curls up very small again
When he grows very tired.

ACTION: Select one, or several, or all children to be Horatio.
Translate words to actions.

See My Candle

See my candle,
Tall and white.
Light the wick,
It's burning bright.

See the flame,
So gently sway.
See the candle
Melt away.

ACTION:
  Verse 1:
    Line: 1 & 2. Stand up straight, arms at side.
          3 & 4. Put arms up in "steeple" fashion above head.
  Verse 2:
    Line: 1 & 2. Sway body.
          3 & 4. Melt body away by gently falling down.

My Umbrella

I have a big umbrella
With colours bright and gay.
It's, oh, so very useful
On a wet and rainy day.

I can skip through splashy puddles,
Or run down to the shop,
I can march just like a soldier,
Or bounce, or jump, or hop!

So, you see, my gay umbrella
Is as useful as can be,
When a sunny day turns rainy
It can be fun for me!

ACTION:
Verse 1: Open and hold up imaginary umbrella.
Verse 2: Do the actions suggested by the words.
Verse 3: Shake rain from umbrella, close it, and skip away.

Funny Freddie Frog

Funny, Freddie, frog,
Does funny, funny tricks!
Like, hop on one leg,
And back-leg kicks.

Funny, Freddie, frog,
What else can you do?
[*Freddie does trick*]
Well anything you can,
We can do too!

ACTION: Select one child to be Freddie. Other children are frogs.
Verse 1: All join Freddie doing tricks.
Verse 2:
   Line: 1 & 2. Children ask Freddie (Freddie does trick). The children follow Freddie saying last two lines.

Elephants

Five little elephants
Standing in a row.
Five little trunks
Waving to and fro.
"Good day," said an elephant, "I must go".
Four little elephants, standing in a row.

Continue with

> Four little elephants ...
> Three little elephants ...
> Two little elephants ...

One little elephant
Standing in a row.
One little trunk
Waving to and fro.
"Good day," said the elephant, "I must go".
No little elephants left in the row.

ACTION: Choose five children to be the "elephants" using arms as trunks. At each verse one little "elephant" leaves the line and returns to the group of onlooking children.

Lets Play Shadows

Lets play shadows,
In the sun.
I can make
My shadow run!

I can make my shadow
Crouch down small,
Or reach up,
Very, very, tall!

I can make my shadow
Jump around,
Or do patterns
On the ground.

My shadow is weary,
See him creep,
Slowly curl up,
Go to sleep.

ACTION: Either translate words to action in full group participation (in the playground on a sunny day); OR
Select individual children to act out each verse, while others observe what the shadows do.

Little Birds

Five little birds
Having a rest,
In the shade of a tall, tall tree.
One little bird spread his wings,
And away flew he!

Continue with

Four little birds ...
Three little birds ...
Two little birds ...

One little bird
Having a rest,
In the shade of a tall, tall tree.
That little bird spread his wings,
And away flew he!

ACTION: Choose five children to be the "birds". One child is the "tree" under which the birds rest. The "tree" stretches her arms horizontally and sways gently. Each bird flies off in turn.

Toy Soldiers

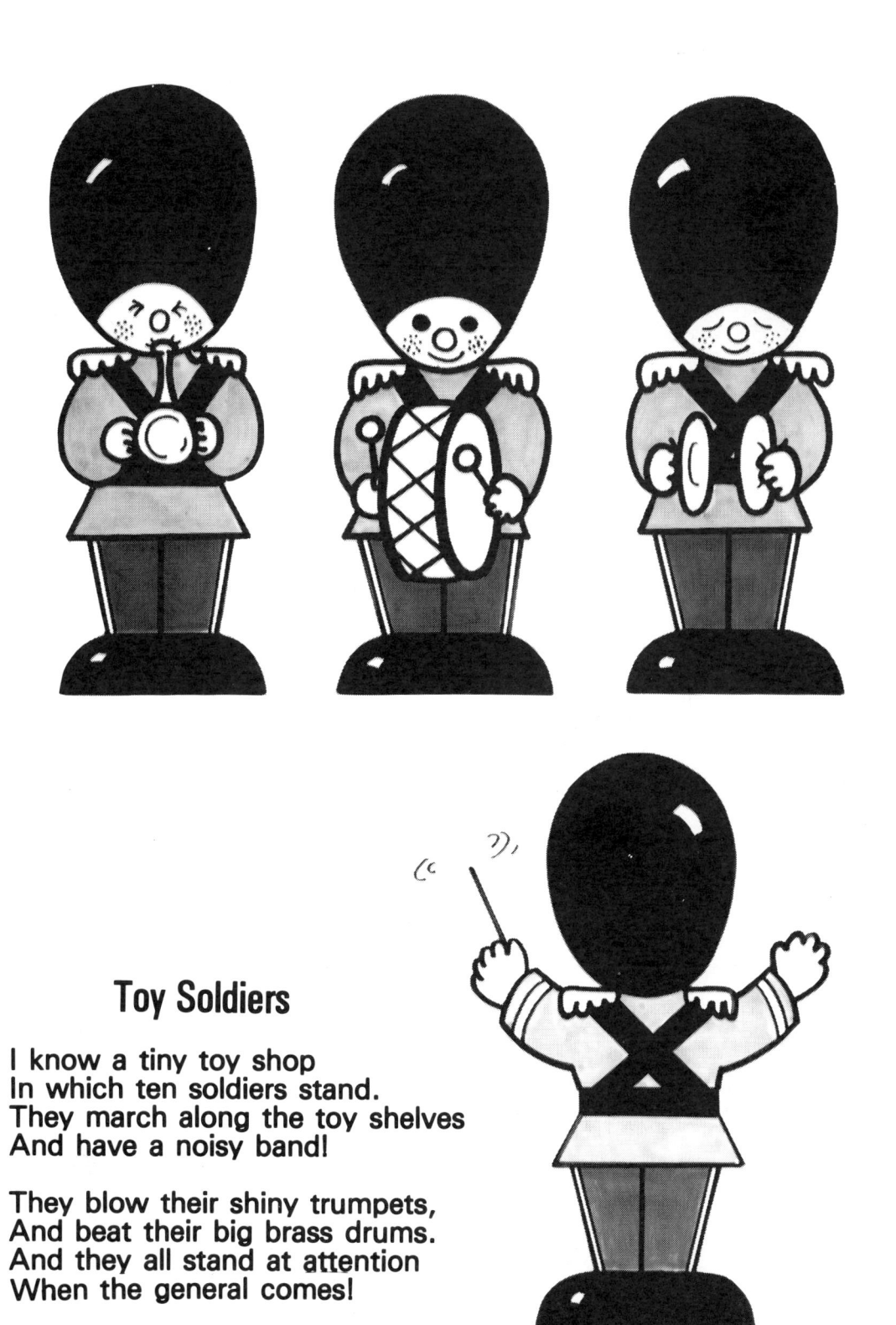

I know a tiny toy shop
In which ten soldiers stand.
They march along the toy shelves
And have a noisy band!

They blow their shiny trumpets,
And beat their big brass drums.
And they all stand at attention
When the general comes!

ACTION: Select a number of children or the whole group to be soldiers and then interpret the words into actions.

Golden Oranges

Golden oranges on the tree,
Ripening in the sun.
A little girl *skipped* by
And she picked one.

Golden oranges on the tree,
Ripening in the sun.
A little boy *ran* by,
And he picked one.

Golden oranges on the tree,
Ripening in the sun.
A little bird *flew* by,
And she picked one.

Golden oranges on the tree,
Ripening in the sun.
A little soldier *marched* by,
And he picked one.

ACTION: Select four children to be "oranges". At each verse a different child is selected to be the "girl skipping", "bird flying", etc.

Fairies In My Garden

Down in my garden
By the old gum tree,
I saw three fairies dancing,
One, two, three.

They made a fairy circle
And skipped and skipped around,
They stooped to pick up daisy chains,
That lay upon the ground.

They held their shiny magic wands
And did a dance so gay,
Then they flapped their fairy wings
And gently flew away.

ACTION: One child (or mother or teacher) is selected to read the verse. Three children or the whole group are fairies and dramatize the words.

The Circus

This is a seal
With a ball on his nose.

This is a chimp on his tricycle
Round and round he goes!

Here is the elephant
Blowing water so high,

And the tight-rope walker
Is up in the sky!

The ponies trot around and out,
The band is playing too.

The ringmaster has cracked his whip—
He says goodbye to you.

ACTION: A single child can depict all the characters and translate words into actions, or individual children can be the different characters directed by a "ringmaster".

Five Little Flowers

Five little flowers,
So gay and bright—
Some were pink and
Some were white.
Along came a little girl [*or boy*]—*give name*
With a brand new cent,
Bought one little flower,
And away she went.

Continue with

Four little flowers ...
Three little flowers ...
Two little flowers ...

One little flower
So gay and bright—
It was pink and
It was white.
Along came a little boy
With a brand new cent,
Bought the last flower,
And away he went.

ACTION: Choose five children to be "flowers" and place them in a flower stall. Select one child to be the shopkeeper. As each name is called the child goes up to the shopkeeper with a cent and buys a "flower".

Autumn Leaves

Up in a tree
Five brown leaves hung.
When the wind came along,
They swung and swung.
Suddenly, without a sound,
One little leaf
Fell to the ground.

Continue with   Four brown leaves ...
Three brown leaves ...
Two brown leaves ...

Up in a tree
One brown leaf hung.
When the wind came along,
It swung and swung.
Suddenly, without a sound,
The last little leaf
Fell to the ground.

ACTION: Select five children to be the "leaves" and respond to the verse. Each falls down in turn. Equally suitable as a finger play.

The Elf

I am the elf
From the Bottlebrush tree,
Pray, *little girl,*
Will you come with me?

Let's *skip* to the shady old Gum tree
And then to that bush, all alone.
Twice round the Golden Acacia,
Now, *skippety skip* back home.

I am the elf
From the Bottlebrush tree,
Pray, *little boy,*
Will you come with me?

Let's *march* to the shady old Gum tree
And then to that bush, all alone.
Twice round the Golden Acacia,
Then *march, march, march* back home.

ACTION: Select an "elf". He skips to group of children and chooses a little girl to skip around the garden with him, visiting all the trees, etc., depicted by small chairs or other children. He then chooses a boy, action is same as before.

SOME SILLY VERSE

The Emu

The Emu ate my sandwich,
That really wasn't funny!
Because, you see, that left me
With a very rumbly tummy!

The Elephant

Atishoo, said the elephant.
Do you suppose,
I could use your handerchief
To wipe my runny nose!?

The Monkey

Chomp, said the monkey.
Bananas to eat!
I'll wear banana skins
On my little monkey feet!

The Centipede

A centipede with many feet,
Had problems with his toes,
Because you see, in winter time,
They nearly always froze!